# Out of Hiding

## A Memoir of Retreat & Return

# Maya Robinson

**Out of Hiding**
*A Memoir of Retreat and Return*



First edition, 2026
Printed in the United States of America

Published by **Obedient Author**
An imprint of **Obedient Life Enterprises**
www.obedientauthor.org

ISBN: 9798234072559

—

# Dedication

I want to thank **Jesus Christ** for restoring the divine ebb and flow that allowed me to pen this book. My journey has not been easy, and writing this book asked me to return to places I once tried to leave behind and ignore. Yet, even in the hardest seasons, this book has reminded me just how close He's always been. Thank you, Jesus, for not allowing me to drift too far away.

To Mom and Dad, you are the foundation of everything I am and know. It has been a gift to be your daughter. The wisdom, love, and grounding you have poured into me have shaped who I am, and your steady presence has helped me return to myself when I felt deeply lost. Thank you for never giving up on me and committing to lead, guide, and parent me. I love you beyond words.

To my future husband, thank you for pushing me forward and helping me see who I am when my vision was too blurry to believe it myself. Thank you for speaking into my heart, my life, and holding my hand as I completed this project. Thank you for being my greatest advocate and cheerleader. You are God's greatest gift to me. I love you.

To my community of sister-friends, your presence in my life has healed and restored the joy and hope of friendship in me. Thank you for doing life with me!

And to you, the reader. Thank you for taking the time to hear my heart, sit with my thoughts, and receive my story. I pray this book helps you see your own story through a clearer lens. My prayer is that as you read, you recognize that you can come out of hiding, and that there is something greater waiting for you beyond any hurt, pain, or disappointment you have experienced in your past.

# Table of Contents

"Come out of hiding, you're safe here with Me.
There's no need to cover what I already see.
You've got your reasons, but I hold your peace.
You've been on lockdown, but I hold the key."

*- Out of Hiding x Steffany Gretzinger, Amanda Cook, Bethel Music*

# Foreword

## Dr. Bettina Robinson

Some stories are written simply to be read. Others are written because they must be told. As a mother, there are moments when you begin to recognize that your child carries something special, something that cannot be taught, manufactured, or fully explained. It is simply the hand of God on their life.

Maya is our middle child, our baby girl. From very early on, I could see that she was deeply sensitive, loving, and caring. There was always a depth to her, a quiet awareness and inquisitiveness that was rare for someone her age. Over time, that sensitivity grew into a beautiful gift. Maya has always carried a natural grace for caring for others and connecting with people. There is something almost magnetic about her presence; people are drawn to her without effort. Her compassion and concern for others reflect the very heart of God, and it is that same heart that now flows through the way she cares for others.

Even as a young girl, it was clear to me that God had placed something special within her life. But as is often the case with those who carry a genuine calling, the path has not always been easy.

*Out of Hiding* is Maya's honest and courageous account of her journey from hurt to healing. In these pages, she shares openly about moments in her life that were painful and confusing, moments that attempted to break her confidence, distort her identity, and challenge her ability to trust herself and others. Yet, what you will discover in this book is not only the story of pain. It is also the story of resilience and healing.

Maya allows you, the reader, to walk with her through the difficult but necessary process of confronting wounds, walking through forgiveness, rediscovering her voice, and reclaiming the identity God placed within her from the very beginning. Her transparency is both brave and deeply meaningful because it reminds us that healing is not something we arrive at overnight. It is something we pursue daily with honesty, faith, and the help of God.

As her mother, I have watched her grow through every season, both the beautiful ones and the hard ones. What I admire most about Maya is not only the gift she carries but the courage she has shown in allowing God to heal the places that tried to silence her.

My prayer is that as you read this book, you will see that Maya's story is not just her own. Many of us have experienced seasons where life tried to push us into hiding. Where pain, disappointment, or brokenness made us question who we are and who God created us to be.

But healing has a way of calling us back into the light. This book is an invitation to step out of hiding and into truth, into healing, and into the purpose God has always had for your life.

Maya, your dad and I are incredibly proud of you, not just for the woman you are steadily becoming, but for the courage it took to share your story. I believe your voice will help many find the strength to reclaim their own.

*"You are the light of the world. A city set on a hill cannot be hidden." Matthew 5:14*

**Your Proud Momma,
Bettina Robinson**

# **Chapter 1: Kept**

We were living in Minnesota then. I remember parts of my childhood townhome. The narrow staircase, the large windows, and the snow that seemed to quiet the whole neighborhood in winter. We moved there in 1993 so my father could finish his postdoc at the University of Minnesota. Dad spent long hours in the lab and on campus, while my mom stayed home with my sister, 18 months older, and me. There is a pivotal story my parents have always shared about that time.

They said the day began like any other. I was one year old, laughing and playing in the living room with my sister. All of a sudden, without a word, I walked over to the couch and laid my head on the pillow. Mom watched me for a moment, trying to figure out what had changed. She thought, *"What's wrong with my baby?"* She called my name. "Maya." No response. I just lay there. She came closer, picked me up, and I laid my head on her shoulder. When she looked at me, she noticed my fair skin cheeks were red and the inside of my lips had turned dark blue.

Immediately, she called my dad at the lab and told him something was wrong. He came home right away and together they rushed me to the emergency room where they learned their one-year-old was in the middle of a severe asthma attack. It was critical and life-threatening. My parents were in shock. They hadn't even known I had asthma. There had been no signs, no warnings, no preparation. Just a sudden fight for breath.

The emergency room staff initiated breathing treatments, but my lungs wouldn't open. They then discovered fluid had built up, making the treatment ineffective, and immediately called for an ambulance to rush me to Fairview Children's Hospital for more intensive care.

Upon arrival, I was immediately placed on 100% oxygen. My lungs were unable to function on their own. Each day, my parents prayed over me, rocked me, and petitioned to the Lord to deliver their child. Church members visited to do the same. As my parents recall, I was quiet and lethargic. I wanted to play, but my body wouldn't allow it. By day two, as my body began to respond to treatment, the oxygen was decreased to 80%. The kind nurses brought popsicles and checked on me every few hours to make sure I was responding well to the treatments.

By the third day, the oxygen was decreased to 50%. I was given a chance to go to the children's playroom, and my oxygen support was further reduced to 30%. By the time I returned from the playroom, it was confirmed that I no longer needed oxygen. The medical staff kept me an additional day to ensure I could breathe on my own. By the fourth day, I could, and I was discharged.

The medical staff informed my parents that I was a miracle because "I was a sick little girl." However, when we left the hospital, my life was very different. From that point on, albuterol nebulizer treatments and steroids became a normal part of my life. My parents watched me closely, ready to act at any sound of wheezing or shortness of breath. That rhythm carried through my childhood from 1993 to 1998 until, slowly, my lungs strengthened and no longer needed assistance.

I don't remember those moments of critical condition, but that moment in Minnesota sits at the beginning of my story like a marker, proof that my being here has always carried intention. For my parents, I was the child they almost lost but was **kept.**

Sometimes that's how purpose has to be remembered. Through the eyes of those who saw what we couldn't see or understand yet. My parents remembered the blue in my face. They remembered the fear. They remembered how close everything came to ending. And they remembered that I was delivered.

There is something sacred about them holding that memory for me, in the way other people can sometimes recognize the weight of your life before you ever learn to recognize it yourself. To have people in your life who remember *you were, indeed, kept*.

*Even if you don't remember how. Even if you don't know why, and even if you don't feel it yet.* **You were. And it was for a reason.**

That's what my parents did for me, without ever saying those exact words. And I believe that's why I've been led to write this, for you. Not to convince you of anything. Not to perform healing or pretend everything has been easy. But to **remember with you.** To hold the memory of your significance while you reconnect to it. To say gently, there has always been meaning here. Even when you didn't see it. Even when you forgot. Even when life knocked the breath out of you and made you quiet.

I would like to hold the reminders for you until the remembering returns. If you can't **sense** the fullness of your purpose yet, that's okay. But you have been kept and something in you is ready to breathe again. To come out of hiding.

# Chapter 2: Dealing with the Difference

## From Safety to Scrutiny

I remember being the child who just felt DIFFERENT. Not only dealing with a sickness that set me apart from my brother and sister, but I also felt different in personality, temperament, and physical appearance. I noticed early on that I was physically different from my immediate family. Everyone else was slender or average-sized, something widely accepted in Western culture, while I was the only full-figured one. According to my mom, the steroids I was prescribed for asthma contributed to my adolescent weight gain. I was the only plus-size in my immediate family, but my family never commented on my extra little pudges. Home was a safe haven, filled with warmth and acceptance.

My dad, a biological scientist, and my mom, an HR professional, both saved and ministry-minded, created an environment that felt like home, not just a house. I don't remember many, if any, instances where my parents pointed out our physical differences; instead, they highlighted our commonalities. All three of us were often celebrated for our shared dimples, which my dad humorously referred to as "our muscle defects." I grew up in a home where physical attributes weren't criticized. We were all equal but unique in our differences. However, leaving the safety of my home was often shocking to my system, as the outside world was very good at pointing out anything DIFFERENT. The moment I stepped outside that protected environment, my difference stopped being something I noticed but became something I had to navigate.

I recall shopping for school attire with my sister and mom, searching in vain for the same hot pink polo my slim-figured sister found with ease. I was often frustrated at the thought of having to go shopping. To know what you're looking for, to need it, but it never being made available to you was a crushing blow to self-esteem. The embarrassment of having to buy men's polos to meet the school's dress code because there weren't options for heavier children was sometimes unbearable. I remember squeezing into the only XXL Aeropostale hoodie available, desperately wanting to coordinate outfits like the other girls at school. I wore that poor hoodie out, because I wanted to wear the clothes that I thought were nice, but they simply did not exist for me because of my size.

As early as seven or eight years old, I remember my weight becoming a topic of conversation outside my household. I recall going to extended family gatherings during the holidays and hearing people exclaim, "You're losing weight, Maya!" Weight loss began to be praised, even though I was never on any type of weight-loss plan. My body was ebbing and flowing as it was designed to during adolescence.

Those comments embedded a deep insecurity that surfaced around certain parts of my family. I never spoke about it, but I learned how to silently endure. I always knew I was beautiful, yet I felt like my beauty was docked because of my weight. And it wasn't just clothes and comments that felt like infractions. Every corner of my childhood reminded me that my body required accommodations life wasn't prepared to make for me.

Shoe shopping was another struggle. On Sundays, I would need those extra five to ten minutes to force my size 11 foot into the only shoes I could find at Payless or Shoe Show. The entire house would have to wait while my dad pulled out a tablespoon or shoehorn to help me get my left foot in, almost religiously. I shot up to around 5'9" and currently stand at 5'10" in height. Imagine the added struggles of trying to find clothing that now needed to meet your extraordinary height on top of everything else. Everything about my being was DIFFERENT.

These small, everyday battles piled onto each other, shaping how I saw myself long before I had the language for insecurity or identity. ***When your difference creates struggles and makes you feel less than, ostracized, or excluded, it can shift from something you lean into to something you try to run away*** *from*. Being in a constant fight for inclusion and normalcy can make difference feel more like a burden than a blessing. Other parts of who I was drew attention just as loudly, and sometimes even more painfully.

## When Difference Became Duty

Not only did my physical appearance bring attention to me outside of home, but my temperament and maturity did as well. I want to begin by saying, I firmly believe in not adultifying children before their time. I often exhibited maturity beyond my years. My body developed early, and my mental processing was advanced, too. However, I found myself in situations where my maturity led to responsibilities I wasn't prepared for nor desired to carry. At school, that "maturity" was interpreted as readiness, and readiness quickly became responsibility

I remember being asked in grade school to reach up and grab things from the top shelves for my teachers and classmates. I realized I never enjoyed being made to stand out that way. Something in me would shrink as everyone watched me grab the box of pencils off the top shelf. While they praised me for completing the task, I could almost feel a cape being put on my back that I never wanted to wear. However, I leaned into it because, in some way, it made me feel needed and, for once, included.

I was often tasked with supervising my classmates when my teacher left the room. At first, it felt empowering to be in charge. Looking back, I see that I was consistently put in a position to govern others when I really needed guidance myself.

In grade school, the line system was a way to keep children orderly, with two coveted positions: the line leader and the caboose. If you were made line leader, you were hot stuff. The caboose, while important, was always last. I was often designated the caboose because of my height, and I hated it. Once again, another responsibility hinged on my difference. It was one I didn't want but accepted because it made me feel included and important outside of my home. This was the inception point of the belief that my belonging was tied to my performance. The more I could do for others, the more I would be included and valued. And just when I thought difference had exhausted its categories, another layer emerged, one that shaped me in ways I felt no one around me fully understood.

## The Divine Difference

I was a highly sensitive and spiritual child with an interest in the Lord. I often felt like I had no one to talk to about God. My sister, eighteen months older, was carving out her independence; something I didn't understand then, but as an adult, I now recognize as the eldest daughter's need to individuate. My younger brother was born five years after me, and that age gap came with its own preset distance.

I was often alone with my own thoughts and found ways to insulate myself, in ways only middle children understand. God and the things of God truly felt like they found me. That loneliness created space, and in that space, something sacred met me.

I was listening to "Alpha and Omega" by Israel Houghton on my iPod shuffle, a song I later coined as my heart song. As I sat alone on the floor of my room, in front of my newly built double doors, I sensed a sweetness wrapping around me and my heart in a way I'd never felt. Tears streamed down my face profusely. A tingling sensation covered my body. I felt SAFE. Covered. Secure.  Engulfed in love like never before. I was experiencing the tangible presence of the Holy Spirit for the first time, not in a church, but in my childhood room. I sat in that presence and truly knew that God was real for the first time in my life.

The things of God drew me in, not because of the system, but because I had encountered Him. However, while I loved the awareness of God that came with spiritual sensitivity, I didn't enjoy the spotlight that came with it.

**Called Out, Set A Part**

As early as middle school, I was known as "the church girl." I don't recall doing anything explicit to earn that title. I just think when it's on you, it's on you, and there's nothing you can do to shy away from it. I often think about an experience in the seventh or eighth grade with a classmate named Symph in the staircase of Martin Luther King Magnet School. I was standing with her and a group of classmates who cursed like sailors. To be honest, I loved it. I wasn't raised in a household where swearing was the norm. My parents grew up in the backwoods of North Carolina. My father was raised a preacher's kid in a Baptist upbringing. Bona fide independent women raised my mother. Cursing wasn't foreign to them, but our house was a no-cursing zone. We weren't even permitted to say "liar." In Black culture, some words *feel* like curse words, and what followed their use wasn't worth the risk. Respectability and decorum were the standards at home, and my parents taught us that you could have clean fun and still have the time of your life.

In that staircase, surrounded by kids who used cursing as a second language, I decided to try one out for size. I thought, "we're all friends here, right?". I blurted out a sentence with a perfectly placed swear. As soon as the expletive left my mouth, the stairway grew silent. Symph looked at me, befuddled. Her next words caught me off guard, not because they were harsh, but because they pierced a truth I was already carrying.

She asked, "Maya, what are you doing?" Confused, I responded, "What are you talking about?" She answered firmly, "YOU don't do that. That's not you. WE do that. YOU don't." I felt embarrassed. But deep down, what jarred me was that someone noticed my difference and, once again, said, "You don't belong here." She wasn't rude, she was honest, and she was putting me back in the place I belonged, but didn't desire to be in. DIFFERENCE.

# Chapter 3: Before the Shrinking

My parents would often brag about how creatively inclined I was as a child, specifically musically. They'd tell stories about how I would hum on key and in pitch as a baby, before I could even talk. My dad would exclaim, "This child is on key! And she's not even talking yet!"

My grandparents would tell me how my sister had her own announcement system for my wakeups. Apparently, she would call out to the house, *"Mina Bird woke!"* because she could hear me humming from my crib beside hers. I earned the nickname "Bird" from my grands partly because I was always humming or singing, and partly because when food came around, I would open my mouth like a baby bird ready to be fed. For the record, Bird is strictly reserved for family usage only. It appears here for storytelling purposes and nothing more.

Creativity and connection came naturally to me. Creative freedom felt less like thinking and more like doing. Less hesitation and more movement. In my body, it felt like adventure, not burden. I didn't overanalyze. I didn't pause. I didn't ask for permission. I just did. And that doing made me feel alive.

When I think of younger Maya, the first image I see is a girl who simply flowed into the things she wanted to do. In elementary school, when I decided I wanted to be a culinary artist, I went for it. Mom and Dad purchased Reynolds cookbooks and all the baking tools a girl could ask for. I experimented, baked, mixed, and created because it brought me joy. I wasn't waiting to be perfect, and my dishes were the epitome of less than perfect. Which is ironic because, to this day, cooking is not my forte. But like the age-old tale says, you never know until you try.

One of my earliest favorite creative memories is from elementary school. I had learned the ending dance scene from *Sister Act II* and told my teacher, Mrs. Love, about it. She asked me to teach it to her after school. My payment? A box of Girl

Scout Samoas. Getting paid for doing something that came naturally to me was a no-brainer! I asked for permission and coordinated pickup with my parents, stayed after class, and taught her the dance so she could teach it to her church dance team. The pride I felt from that moment was palpable. Mrs. Love made me and my creativity feel important, seen, and necessary.

Middle school was where my creativity and tenacity began to take on new life. I remember running for class vice president and came up with a full campaign slogan: *"Vote for Maya, She's on Fiya."* Determined to beat the competition, I wrapped white labels around pencils with the campaign name printed on them, stuffed them in little bags, and handed them out like campaign merchandise. That, along with my convincing PowerPoint presentation, allowed me to win by a landslide. I was no match for my opponents.

My confidence grew to new heights during those middle school years. I'll never forget auditioning for our school's basketball-game dance team. I was often silently apprehensive about my physical abilities, but something in me knew I had to audition. I remember staying after school to audition and waiting with bated breath the next day for the results to be posted. When I saw my name in bold, MAYA ROBINSON, on that posted white sheet of paper, I was ecstatic. I had proven to myself that I was capable, despite my physical insecurities. And when I put on my blue sequined top, black bell-bottom dance pants, and dance shoes, you couldn't convince me I wasn't Beyonce! Performing our first routine to Snoop Dogg's "Drop It Like It's Hot" and T.I.'s "Bring 'Em Out" felt like magic. Dancing alongside my peers and in front of the crowds made me feel like I *finally* fit somewhere.

My musicality deepened during those middle school years, too. I was always singing, listening, dissecting songs, figuring out harmonies, and developing my ear without even realizing it. I came from a musically inclined family. My dad sang in a quartet group called Sons of the Silvergates during his younger years, and music has always been the glue that bonded our family. By thirteen, I was singing in church behind seasoned vocalists, invited to join adult choirs, picking up arrangements quickly, and learning how to listen and lead simultaneously.

High school expanded my creative world even more. I played clarinet and often held first or second chair. I joined church dance teams, participated in cotillions, and began to experiment with beauty. I always had a natural knack for hair, but high school was when I honed it more professionally. I took cosmetology classes, earning hours toward a full cosmetology license while still a teenager. I became skilled with makeup, learning techniques and mastering looks long before social media made it an industry.

By late high school and early college, fashion and beauty became a major creative outlet for me. Thrifting became my pastime because it was one of the few fashion spaces where size didn't limit possibilities. When something didn't exist, I created it. I remember turning long-sleeved shirts into pencil skirts, crafting outfits out of whatever I could find. I was resourceful, determined, and expressive in every direction.

But what I loved most about myself creatively back then was that I was fearless. I was curious. I didn't overthink. I tried first and refined later based on what I learned. That version of me was ambitious and bold. Whatever it was, I went for it.

I didn't yet know that the world would one day teach me to judge my own creativity. I didn't yet know that self-doubt could silence expression or that comparison could poison joy. At that time, creation was just creation. Not performance, not pressure, not perfection. Just me, free.

And just like there were countless moments that made me feel free, there were also countless moments that began to shape my shrinking. It wasn't one rupture. It was dozens of tiny ones. Barely noticeable at the time, but sharp enough to leave dents. A look here. A suggestion there. A silence. A comment that lingered longer than it should have. Those were the beginnings. The quiet places where I started to pull back, second-guess, rehearse, and overthink. I didn't know it yet, but this was the start of my shrinking.

14

# Chapter 4: The Slow Retreat

The slow retreat didn't announce itself. It didn't feel like fear or insecurity at first. It felt like awareness; a sudden consciousness of myself in ways I'd never experienced. One moment I was moving freely, and the next I was watching myself move, adjusting, shrinking by degrees too subtle to name. That's how it began. Not with a single wound, but with several whispers.

**Retreat doesn't always look like running. Sometimes it looks like overthinking. Sometimes it looks like politeness. Sometimes it looks like silence.** The slow retreat, for me, looked like becoming hyperaware of every part of myself. My body, my voice, my presence, my difference. I didn't know I was pulling back. I only knew it felt safer than being fully seen.

## Censored Sensitivity

Some children move through the world untouched by what they cannot see, but I was not one of them. I felt everything: atmospheres, shifts, fear, tension, and even the emotions people thought they were hiding. My spirit responded long before my mind understood what it was reacting to. I did not have language for discernment or spiritual sensitivity at that age, but those qualities were already shaping how I experienced the world.

One of the first times I realized how deeply I felt things was during the events surrounding the 9/11 attacks. I was a child, far too young to comprehend the details of what was happening, yet the weight of it sank into me in a way that felt heavier than anything I had ever known. The entire country was afraid, but the fear settled into me with a depth I could not explain. Something stirred inside me that I did not know how to articulate, and it stayed with me for weeks.

During that time, I often found myself awake at night. It was not restlessness or insomnia. Something in me has always been wired for the nighttime, almost as if the quiet hours open a channel of awareness that the daytime blurs. But this was different.

During that time period, I would lie in my room with my face pressed into a pillow so my parents could not hear me cry. I felt overwhelmed by what was happening in the world, but I did not know how to express the size of the fear and uneasiness I felt. I only knew that something in me was trembling. I began having dreams of raids and attacks. To a third grader, they were nightmares. But when I look back, I believe I was sensing what the world would soon witness out loud.

That same sensitivity followed me into school. During the brief period when I attended public school, the environment felt spiritually loud and emotionally chaotic. Kids my age were already stepping into provocative choices, and although I was friends with them, something in the atmosphere unsettled me in a way I could not understand at the time. **I carried the weight of what I sensed long before I ever spoke a word of it.**

One moment stands out clearly. I remember walking with a group of girls to the cafeteria, a dim and drab room that always felt heavy to me. We sat at a round table, and almost immediately the girls reached into their backpacks. Instead of pulling out notebooks or snacks, they pulled out condoms and began passing them around casually, as if it were nothing at all. I was in the fifth grade. Shock moved through me, but beneath it was a deeper sorrow. A grief I felt in my spirit before I could name it. Something about that moment marked me, and it has stayed with me ever since.

In the days that followed, I began arriving at school in tears. I carried a frustration that I could not articulate, but the heaviness showed up every morning. My teacher noticed and eventually called a parent-teacher conference. She believed something must have been happening at home. But home was fine. The turmoil lived inside me. I was absorbing the atmosphere around me without knowing how to give voice to any of it.

People often labeled me sensitive or sheltered, but neither description captured what was actually happening. I was not sheltered. I was spiritually aware. I was discerning even as a child.

I felt things intensely, long before I could explain them, and because I did not yet have the vocabulary for what I sensed, my reactions were regularly misunderstood.

When you perceive deeply in a world that prefers surface level, your sensitivity becomes easy for others to misinterpret. And when it is misinterpreted long enough, you begin to question the parts of yourself that were never wrong. I took on labels like sensitive and sheltered, and even though they were not true, they clung to me. They shaped how I saw myself and made me believe I was somehow broken. The truth was that I was simply responding to life in a deeper way. My sensitivity was not the flaw. The misunderstanding of it was the hindrance. What became censored was not my feelings, but my confidence in the way I was created to be.

## A Place Where I Could Soar

My family's roots are in North Carolina, but because of my dad's research and occupation as a biological professor, we landed in Tennessee in 1998 when my dad accepted an offer for full professorship at Tennessee State University. For my dad, regardless of the city we were in, we needed to have a church home. We attended two churches during the first few years in Nashville, but something always felt *off* about the ministry. Nothing seemed like the right fit.

One day, a few of my dad's students began raving about this new church in the Nashville area. They emphatically talked about this preacher who led the youth ministry at the time, and their proclamations convinced Dad to visit. In true Dad fashion, he visited a weekday Bible study on his own before bringing the rest of us.

During his visit, he was able to hear the youth pastor his students were raving about and was highly impressed, which, for Dad, is a tough feat to accomplish. Soon after his initial visit, we attended as a family. I remember it like it was yesterday. We left the church service, and Dad began polling us, asking what we thought about it. He asked our opinions on the people, the atmosphere, and our time with the youth ministry. Unanimously, we said we liked it and felt we wanted to stay. After visiting for a few months, we joined the church. My parents have always been serious about the things of the Lord and carry a God-given gift for connecting with people. Naturally, our family quickly became immersed in the ministry and began to draw people.

When we joined this church, it felt like finding oxygen for me. Their youth ministry was vibrant and alive. For the first time, I wasn't the *only* one. For the first time, I didn't feel strange. I didn't feel "too much." I felt at home. As the child who felt drawn to God in a way that didn't always match the world around me, that difference set me apart early. But I didn't have a place to land with it. Not at school. Not even always at home. I didn't have a community of kids my age who understood what it meant to feel everything spiritually, to be sensitive to things no one else was paying attention to, to love God deeply without really knowing why. This ministry filled that void for me. I could leave school, where I was always aware of my differences, and come into a space where those differences felt purposeful.

I felt connected, seen, and open. On top of that, I met my best friend, the pastor's son. We bonded instantly over music, over harmonies, over the way worship felt like a place we both could breathe. He became one of my safe spaces, and I believe I was one for him too.

He was one of the first people who understood the way my heart worked and how my mind ticked. He came from a pretty well-off family and had a car by the time he turned 15. He'd pick me up on weekends, come by my house with burnt cd's of music he wanted me to have and listen to. I knew that anytime I received a cd, a follow-up conversation was coming to dissect what I liked and disliked. He was my friend through and through, and I didn't have to perform around him. It was amazing to not only find a place where you belong but also find a friend who gets you at the same time. He wasn't half bad looking either. It was awesome, and I truly believed we'd be in that place forever.

Because my parents became immersed in the ministry and given leadership roles, we were at church a lot. Bible studies. Rehearsals. Youth nights. Weekend services. Special events. You name it, we were there. From the ages of thirteen to eighteen, the church became the place where I felt I could soar. A place where my voice mattered. Where my sensitivity wasn't strange. Where my creativity had room. It was the place where my voice developed, not just in singing but in the things of the Lord. For a while, it was everything I needed. Until it wasn't.

### Retreating at the Retreat

One of the moments that has stayed with me happened during a summer youth retreat our church took us on. We were piled into a seven-passenger van heading four hours outside of Nashville to a private lodge the youth ministry had reserved. I can still picture the way we were arranged inside that van: knees pressed against seats, backpacks tucked under legs, and our bodies shifting with each turn on the interstate. The windows were cracked just enough to let the warm summer air move through, and the counselors were doing their best to keep us entertained. Conversations overlapped in every direction. Music played in the background. Laughter filled the spaces between sentences. Everything felt loud and alive.

I remember feeling open, curious and comfortable in that van. I asked questions about God and the Spirit of the Lord, questions that had been sitting in my heart for a long time. They came out of me naturally, not as a performance and not because I wanted attention, but because I genuinely wanted to understand. Somewhere in the middle of all that conversation, I heard one of the counselor's comments in a tone that blended affection with exhaustion. She snickered, "I love her intuitiveness, but if this girl asks one more question..." The words drifted into the air and settled inside me before I could fully process them. Even though they were spoken lightly, they landed harshly.

I have always believed that the moments that stay with us deserve attention. They linger because they are revealing something, even if we do not recognize it right away. People often learn to ignore those internal alarms, to brush off the sting and move on, but I eventually learned that the moments that cling the longest are the ones that carry lessons about God, about ourselves, and about the people who shape us.

That van ride remains vivid in my memory because I believe it was one of the first times I felt pressure to adjust how I operated. Something inside me pulled inward, not dramatically but subtly, as if a quiet voice suggested that my natural curiosity might be too much. Until that moment, I had never viewed my way of thinking or the way I processed spiritual things as a burden or annoyance. After that comment, however, I became more aware of how I sounded, how often I spoke, and how deeply I wanted to understand things that did not interest most kids my age.

Later in life, I realized how easily that small internal shift spread into other areas. I often wondered if I was too much, questioning whether I needed to soften my personality and constantly considered if I needed to quiet myself so others would not feel overwhelmed by me. What I believed to be minor self-adjustments at the time were actually early signs of retreat for me.

That day in the van marked one of the first moments where I folded a part of myself inward. It was small enough that no one around me would have noticed, but it carried enough weight to take root.

### A Church that Hurt

Everything shifted with the church when my mom stepped into an assignment God had given her: a women's empowerment conference built around her book, *What About Me.* It was a work born from years of carrying others, leading with integrity, and navigating the quiet ache of being a woman who served God devoutly, yet was often overlooked. My mom had served in ministry for years and, at this point, was the only woman elder in the church; a title rarely given to women in the traditional structures of ministry, yet a responsibility she held with honor and consistency.

Because the church culture operated with a strong expectation that nothing should be done outside its walls without pastoral awareness, my mom shared her heart with the pastor. She told him about the book, mentioned that she had included him in the dedication, and asked if he would open the conference with remarks. He agreed. Everything appeared to be in alignment. But when the conference weekend arrived, he did not show up.

We were surprised, but we kept going. The conference weekend unfolded beautifully. Women encountered breakthroughs. The atmosphere was full, and Mom poured out with grace and conviction. Our family had traveled from North Carolina to support her, and the weekend felt like a culmination of everything she had carried quietly for years. When it ended, we were full, grateful, and exhausted. By Sunday morning, we had no more to give. Hosting family and managing a full conference took everything out of us. But my mom, being who she had always been, insisted we still go to church. Commitment has always lived in her bones. Even tired, even stretched, she showed up.

Because we were late and had family with us, she chose not to sit in the designated elder section. Instead, we found seats on the youth side. As we walked in, people who had attended the conference stopped her to say how powerful it was and how much the *What About Me* conference had spoken to them. We were grateful for the warmth and genuine gratitude in those exchanges. As we settled into our seats, we believed it would be a normal Sunday.

The pastor walked up to the pulpit, and I will never forget the way he began his sermon. With a smile and tone that suggested nothing was wrong, he said, "I heard it was a great time this weekend." I remember feeling a flash of confusion. A small pause inside myself. I even wondered if maybe the men had held a breakfast or some event I hadn't known about, because as far as the women's conference…how would he know? He wasn't there.

Before I had time to make sense of it, his tone began to shift and so did his sentiments. The warmth faded, his posture changed, and the next sentence did not match the one before it. It was as if he used that opening line as a doorway into something entirely opposite. Without naming her, he began speaking about people who "tried to be bigger than the house." People who "did things outside the ministry and couldn't even show up on Sunday." People who "forgot order." Each line landed with offense and intention. Each word was pointed. Each insinuation drew a straight line to my mother, even though he never dared to say her name.

The room tightened. His words were public and designed to humiliate. What he didn't know was that my mom was sitting right there, hearing every word. I remember the confusion on the choir stand. The sideways glances. The quiet shifting of people trying to figure out what was happening. The same people who celebrated her were now nodding along, pretending not to witness the injustice unfolding in front of them. It was the first time I witnessed a spiritual leader harm someone under the guise of authority. And it stunned me. I'll never forget my great aunt who was attending for the very first time, whispering a very Baptist, "Oh hell no." Mom, in all of her grace, gently put her hand on her leg and mouthed, "Don't you dare." She knew they were not the type to sit and allow disrespect to go unaddressed. But we sat there. We stayed.

The pastor proceeded with his sermon and began to take an offering following his close. My mom asked me for a dollar. She walked to the front, placed it in the basket, and looked him directly in the eyes. I'll never forget the look on his face as he dropped his head in shame. When the altar call came, she went up again. It was clear she was giving him a chance and an opportunity to correct himself. He placed his hand on her and prayed briefly. When she turned around and left the altar, she caught my eye, lifted her finger, and pointed toward the door. It was time to go. We never stepped foot back into that church.

My dad was not in attendance that morning. He was traveling to take my sister and the pastor's son back to their college. They attended the same school, and Dad had agreed to make the trip to ensure they made it back in time for Monday morning classes. When my dad finally returned from his six-hour commute, he came directly to church and was approached by several distraught individuals who had witnessed what took place. As we were leaving, we caught him in the parking lot. The timing was impeccable. My mother turned to him and said, with quiet authority, "You need to get your pastor." Those words carried grief, disappointment, and a line she refused to let anyone cross again.

By the time we reached home, our phones were buzzing with calls and texts. People who had known our family for years, people my parents had counseled, prayed for, supported, and served, were reaching out in disbelief. And then they started showing up. Car after car pulled into our driveway. People filled our living room. Groups stood in the kitchen, whispering, shaking their heads, trying to make sense of what they had just witnessed.

This wasn't unusual for our home. Because of the impact my parents had made in the church, people often gravitated toward them. But this time was different. This time, they came with grief, shock, confusion, and a kind of collective heartbreak. The betrayal wasn't subtle. It was seen by hundreds of people, and many of them were shaken by it. Some cried. Some apologized even though they weren't the ones at fault. Some kept repeating, "I can't believe he did that." Others said, "We've never seen anything like this." Everyone was looking to my parents for clarity, for leadership, for next steps. But the truth was, we were all trying to process the blow in real time.

As the commotion continued, I snuck off to the bathroom, a place I've always felt safest. I closed the door and cried in a way I had never cried before. I was in disbelief. Something I trusted had shattered. Then my phone rang. It was *him*. The pastor's son. My best friend. The person who understood parts of me most people never even saw. The one I harmonized with, laughed with, grew up with, and trusted without reservation. I answered, and before I could steady myself, he asked quietly, almost urgently, "Maya… what happened?"

There was no accusation in his voice. Just hurt and confusion. A boy caught between loyalty and love in ways he shouldn't have had to be. I told him everything. What happened in that sanctuary. How blindsided and humiliated we were. How his father spoke in ways that didn't align with the man I thought I knew. I told him honestly, "I don't know what's wrong with your dad."

Then he said, soft, sure and with conviction, "Maya… I love you. You're my best friend and this is not going to come between us." And the thing is…I believed him. Every single word. I believed he would fight for the friendship we built and the bond we had. I believed he would hold steady even if everything around us was shaking. And, for a moment, that belief steadied me.

But what I did not understand yet was that some cracks don't show themselves right away. Sometimes they widen quietly, subtly, and almost politely. Until one day, you look up and realize the divide is too wide to cross. That phone call was tender and sincere, but it was also the beginning of a drift neither of us wanted by choice nor intention.

There were many petitions, calls, texts, and emails sent for my mom to return to the church. But noticeably, not one petition for the pastor to apologize. And that silence said everything.

My dad went back to the church twice after that Sunday. The first time, he returned the key to the church. The second time, to meet with the pastor. He told him plainly that what he had done was wrong, that he had mishandled his authority, that he owed my mother an apology, and that leadership requires accountability. But the pastor refused to make it right.

Even after the chaos of that Sunday, my best friend and I still showed up for each other in the small ways we could in the months to follow. I went to his house to see his sister off to prom. He still texted me and we still checked in on each other. We were both moving around the wound trying not to feel the tension and hoping our friendship could stay untouched while everything around it had fractured. All of this had transpired during my senior year of high school, and when he agreed to go to my senior prom with me, it felt like a sign that maybe we could outrun the fallout. That maybe something good could survive the mess.

But a few weeks before prom, my phone rang. I froze when I saw his name light up my screen. Something in me, that same intuitive knowing I had carried my entire life, whispered, "He's going to tell you he can't go to prom with you." Nervous, I let the phone go to voicemail. He left me a message, and I could tell from his voice what the call was about. His voice sounded heavy, hesitant, and not like him as he asked me to give him a call to discuss something.

I told my parents he had called and that I knew what the call was about. I could see the pain flicker in their eyes. They gently encouraged me to call him back, trying to steady me without making the moment heavier than it already was. I sat down on the couch, phone in hand, and dialed his number. I prepared to use that voice you use when you're trying to brace for impact without letting the heartbreak bleed through your tone.

When he picked up, his voice gave everything away before he even spoke the words. He was usually articulate and rarely lost for words. But not this day. He was hesitant and weighted, searching for the right words to say. He started slowly. "Maya… since my dad is paying for my tux and stuff for prom, he said he feels our parents should talk before I can agree to go." He kept going, trying to explain what made no sense to either of us.

He continued, "So basically…I can't go until our parents meet." The translation was as loud as it was painful: We were being used as collateral in a conflict we didn't create. My chest tightened, and I felt a sense of rejection, embarrassment, and a deep unfairness of it all. I recognized we were being used as leverage by his father, and I refused to give in to the manipulation. I kindly declined the offer, told him I understood, and that I would take my father to prom. He exhaled into the phone. I could hear how much he hated delivering that news, how powerless he felt, and how torn he was between loyalty to me and obedience to a father who was using both of us to make a point.

When we hung up, I sat with a kind of disappointment I had never felt before. It wasn't just that he couldn't come with me. It was that someone I cared about didn't choose me when it mattered. That experience planted something in me. It taught me to be more careful. To guard the places of myself I once offered freely. Without realizing it, I started to build guards around my heart and around who had access to me. Not out of weakness, but out of a desire to protect myself from being heartbroken like that again.

**Another Blow**

The church fallout had cracked something deep in my foundation, and the prom unraveling had introduced me to a kind of disappointment and mistrust I had never experienced before. I went on to college and without fully realizing it, I had started to move even more inward. I was still warm, but definitely more guarded at my core. During my sophomore year of college, a new set of friendships began to emerge that I didn't see coming.

Before I go any further, for the purposes of this chapter, I'll be using alias names to honor the privacy of everyone involved. The moments are true. Only the names have been changed.

It began with a simple connection. An acquaintance of mine had ties to a university outside of Nashville, and one of her worship leader friends, Elias, needed background vocalists for an upcoming church event. I'd built a small reputation in Nashville for singing, especially in the Christian community, so the acquaintance recommended me to Elias. That one recommendation opened the door to a new circle I didn't yet know would shape so much of my young adulthood.

Through Elias, I met Cameron, another singer and worship leader, and our musical chemistry formed instantly. Around that same time, I brought someone else into the fold, Janet. I had known Janet since high school. She was a year younger than me and once told me she was drawn to me in high school after learning I was a Christian and felt she needed to get to know me. She was also a singer and growing as a worship leader at her church at the time. Years later, when the circles began to connect, it felt natural to include her in this new ecosystem forming around music and faith.

Elias, Cameron and Janet would come to my parents' house, sometimes staying until the early morning hours. We would worship, stack harmonies, write, laugh, talk about God, talk about life and lose track of time. It was the first time since the loss of my old church community that I felt that type of belonging again. A belonging rooted in creativity, spirituality, and camaraderie. It felt like something sacred was returning to me.

An old musical director from that former church needed background singers for a Christmas event. Since I was now connected with this circle of singers, we agreed to do it together.

After the performance, we were all sitting in the back green room, adrenaline buzzing with harmonies still ringing in our ears. As I settled into how good our friendship felt, sitting on the couch,

I worked up the courage to ask something I had been thinking about. "What do y'all think about us being a group?", I asked. To my surprise, they all said yes. And in that moment, something clicked. We became more than friends. More than singers. We became a unit. A creative family of sorts. I was not only relieved, but excited. I felt like it was just right.

Shortly after we decided to become a group, my sister introduced me to a friend of hers named Sienna. Sienna was looking for a church home and community in Nashville. She could sing, she loved God, and she was a joy to be around. I introduced Sienna to the other members of our group, and she fit right in. She also sang soprano, which was a relief for me as a soprano who preferred to sing alto.

Not long after Sienna joined the friendship, another singer connected to our circle, Logan. Logan was an incredible worship leader in the city, but he was also just an all-around great guy. Logan was an easy addition and with the six of us, Elias, Cameron, Janet, Sienna, Logan, and me, we suddenly felt like a force. We rehearsed, wrote, worshiped, traveled, served. We laughed until our stomachs hurt, dreamed wildly, prayed boldly and became a known sound around Nashville. We were booked for events, invited to travel and minster, and posted across social media during an era when virality was just beginning. It felt beautiful. It felt purposeful. It felt like God was giving me back exceedingly, abundantly something I thought I had permanently lost.

### A Fault Line

Elias had taken some years off from university and was trying to figure out his next steps. Because we had grown close through music and ministry, it was natural for me to care about what he was navigating. So, I did what my family has always done—helped. I went to my parents and asked if he could come stay with us and transfer to the university I was attending, the illustrious Tennessee State University. In true Robinson fashion, they said yes. They didn't need a long list of reasons. They saw a young man who needed support and responded with the generosity that had always been a part of our home.

Having Elias in the house beautifully shifted things. He felt like an older brother. Like someone who understood the musical, spiritual, creative parts of me without explanation. We cooked together. We laughed and made plans that felt full of purpose. The group was stretching, not just musically but also relationally. With more people came more personalities, and with more personalities came occasional tension. The way those moments were handled revealed something I didn't want to see yet.

Whenever tensions rose, or the group disagreed, or someone needed to step in to restore order, Elias retreated and went quiet. He took a stance that felt like "every man for himself." I can admit, I had high expectations for Elias, being the oldest and the one I believed could stand beside me as I aimed for peace. But that wasn't the case.

Around this time, Sienna and I had grown closer. She seemed level-headed, grounded and safe. One day, we were on the phone talking about group dynamics and how to navigate the growing pains. I told her the truth about how I had been feeling. "I think at some point I need to talk to Elias. I don't like the way he doesn't step in to help, and I don't know about that. Something feels off," I expressed. Back then, I can admit I wasn't the most courageous version of myself. Hard conversations scared me. I didn't know how to approach people with the truth of my feelings without feeling as if it would backfire. So instead of talking to Elias right away, I confided in Sienna. It was a decision I learned so much from and one I regret to this day.

Once I confided in Sienna, something in Elias's behavior changed. At first subtly, then unmistakably. It was gradual, almost quiet, the way distance often is when it's intentional but unspoken. At first, it didn't strike me as strange. He had his own life, his own friends, his own rhythms. But then the pattern sharpened. He was spending more and more time with Sienna, not just casually, but consistently. Hours at her place. Evenings there. Coming home late or not at all. And when he did come home, he carried an air that felt unfamiliar. He wasn't mean or cold. He was withheld.

Eventually, the distance between Elias and I became too obvious to ignore. I reached out to both Elias and Sienna and asked them to come over so we could talk. They arrived to my home together. We sat in my bedroom to chat, I on the chair adjacent from my bed while they both sat on my bed. I began by asking, "Are we okay? I just noticed that something feels off and I wanted to open the door for conversation." Elias, apprehensive, turned his head toward Sienna and asked her, "Can I?"

Those words stopped me cold. I thought, "why was he asking *her* for permission? My first thought was maybe they were in a relationship, because the dynamic was new to me. Sienna gave him a small nod, signaling a yes. Elias looked at me and confessed, "I was on the phone that day you talked to Sienna about how you felt about me. She had me on three-way." Suddenly, everything made sense. Sienna dropped her head as Elias continued to speak. Tears streamed down his face, and in that moment, I saw what I had experienced myself. The brunt force of how deeply words, even unintentionally harmful ones, can land in a person's heart. He shared how surprised he was by what I had felt and how much it hurt to hear it secondhand, especially because he considered me like a sister.

The moments that followed were about clarity and apology for me. Hurting him had never been my intention. I explained where my feelings began and my original intent to speak with him directly when the timing felt right. That experience taught me the importance of discernment, not just honesty. Not every thought needs a witness, and not every feeling needs to be shared with others.

Elias and I were able to make amends. Sienna and I, not so much. I struggled to understand her decision to expose a private conversation, even with her poorly explaining how we all "ended up" on three-way in the first place. Though I remained outwardly present, something in me quietly withdrew. I didn't know what reconciliation would look like, but I also wasn't someone who believed in cutting people off. So, I stayed, committed to the group, committed to moving forward in our agreed-upon mission, even when the fractures were there.

## And It All Falls Down

If there was one thing I took from the experience with Elias, it was the realization of how easily relationships could fracture when feelings went unspoken. But just as I was starting to navigate that lesson, another challenge emerged. This time, it was the tension between Janet and Sienna. From the moment Sienna joined the group, Janet never fully accepted her.

I remember pulling both of them aside to talk and Janet outright saying she didn't want to feel like she had to share her friends. She felt like she had to share attention and was threatened by Sienna's presence. I was shocked by her candidness, but I made it clear that there was enough of us to go around. However, the tension never faded between them. Instead, it turned into something we had to constantly manage.

Eventually, it came to a head during a ministry trip to Chattanooga. We were a Christian group, about to go on stage, and literal minutes before we were supposed to minister, we found ourselves breaking up an altercation between Janet and Sienna. I pulled Sienna aside to calm her down, and Cameron pulled Janet aside to do the same. As I prompted Sienna to breathe, counting down from ten to one in one corner, Cameron was containing Janet's anger in another. The next thing we knew, we were being called on stage to complete our assignment as if nothing had happened.

After that incident, things were never quite the same. Janet began distancing herself from the group. Her behavior shifted in a way that everyone in the group could feel. She began to distance herself, not just emotionally but in every little logistical detail that kept us connected. When we had group text messages about scheduling photo shoots or deciding on promotional items, things we always decided together, Janet's silence became the norm. It wasn't occasional. It was a pattern. Her responses came slower and then not at all. It was clear she was pulling away. Decisions that should have taken a day stretched into weeks. The rest of us felt the subtle strain of waiting on someone who seemed no longer invested.

As Janet's silence grew, I began noticing another shift, this time with Cameron. He and I had always shared a sweet, supportive friendship. We were close, and I truly felt like I had been brought into his life to be a safe space for him. As good friends do, we shared things we didn't share with others, and I valued that bond deeply.

But around the same time Janet was pulling away, Cameron began distancing himself too. It wasn't loud or confrontational, but it was noticeable and it left me confused and deeply unsettled. What stood out wasn't just his distance, it was the shift in energy between Janet and Cameron. It was as if something had formed between them, unspoken but visible. A quiet alignment and a secret that wasn't hidden well. I was learning something about myself in real time. I was learning that I notice energy before I understand intention. That I feel shifts before I'm given explanations. That discernment often arrives as discomfort long before it arrives as clarity.

At the time, I questioned myself. I wondered if I was being "sensitive". If I was reading too much into things. But the pattern was becoming familiar: relationships would change, atmospheres would shift, and my spirit would register it before my mind could catch up. My dream life also spiked at this point. I began having these dreams every night for about three weeks as the energy shift within the group intensified. I didn't feel afraid in the dreams, just alert. Curious. It felt like a warning. I asked my mom and my aunt, who had always covered us in prayer, to pray with me. I told them I didn't know exactly what was coming, but I felt strongly that God was preparing me for something to be revealed. It felt like the Lord had me in a holding pattern for the right time. As much as I wanted clarity immediately, I knew I had to wait. I needed timing. I needed wisdom. I needed covering. I didn't want to confront anyone out of emotion. I wanted truth, and I wanted God in the middle of it. So, I waited until I sensed I was released to bring everyone together.

One day, everyone gathered at my home. I remember sitting in my living room, looking around at people I had traveled with, prayed with, and ministered alongside, and feeling like we were strangers. The room felt heavy and quiet in a way that wasn't peaceful. Sienna and Elias sat beside each other on one couch. Janet and Cameron sat beside each other on another. I sat in a chair alone. Logan was unable to attend.

I opened the floor gently, asking if everyone was okay. I asked what was going on, because I knew I couldn't be the only one noticing the shift. I invited anyone who felt something needed to be addressed to speak. After a brief silence, Sienna spoke directly to Janet about her behavior. It wasn't pretty, but it was necessary. Sienna made her boundaries clear around how she would and would not be treated moving forward. Janet never fully took responsibility for the subtle bullying, but Sienna said what she needed to say.

Elias then took the floor and addressed Janet's ongoing reluctance to participate in group decisions. Elias was someone who valued structure, timeliness, and follow-through. He approached the group with a business mindset majority of the time. By that point, it was clear that Janet's lack of responsiveness was disengagement. We had invested money, time, and resources into the group, and her refusal to contribute input while still benefiting from the collective decisions created strain. Her refusal to participate while benefiting from collective decisions created strain, and Elias wanted answers.

When Janet finally spoke, no one anticipated the turn the conversation would take. She named an offense she claimed to have with our manager, my mother, and the room froze. She explained that she disliked one of our principle marketing images because of how she appeared in it. Then she looked directly at my mother and said, "If it were your daughter, you wouldn't have chosen a photo she was uncomfortable with." She followed it by saying she had spoken to the Lord about it and had forgiven her.

We were stunned. Not just by what she said, but by who she said it to. There was confidence in her posture, as if she believed she had taken the righteous route. But she was wrong.

We all reacted at once, saying, *"She didn't choose the images, we did."* My mother calmly asked us to be quiet so she could respond. She didn't flinch. There was no defensiveness, no offense taken, just clarity.

Without raising her voice, she told Janet she couldn't forgive her for something she hadn't done. Janet looked stunned. My mother continued, gently but firmly, explaining that she had not selected the images. The group had after waiting repeatedly for Janet's input and receiving no response. She made it clear that Janet's frustration wasn't with her. It was with the group's decision and with her own lack of participation in the process that led to it. Then she said plainly: *"So no, you do not and cannot have a problem with me."*

Janet never apologized. Instead, she said, "Well, I've already forgiven you, so I'm okay." The room went quiet. There was no ownership. No acknowledgment of assumption. Just spiritual language used as insulation.

Years later, I learned there is a term for that: spiritual bypassing. It happens when someone uses spiritual language to avoid accountability. It sounds holy, but it bypasses truth. And in that moment, it became clear Janet wasn't interested in reconciliation. She was interested in resolution without responsibility.

As all of this unfolded, my attention kept being drawn elsewhere. I remember sitting there, listening to everything being said, while simultaneously feeling this quiet pull in my spirit that said, *don't miss this. There's still something here that needs to be addressed.* Cameron and I needed to talk.

We had been close up until this point and leading up to this meeting, something had changed. He had begun to pull away. Conversations shortened and distance grew where closeness once lived. When the moment with Janet closed, I turned to Cameron and asked plainly, if there was something I had done to offend him. I told him I had noticed the distance and wanted to understand it. He didn't answer right away. He became visibly uncomfortable, and you could see him deciding how much truth he was willing to allow out.

When he finally began to speak, it felt as though I had an earpiece in, like the ones news correspondents wear, where questions were being fed to me in real time by the Holy Spirit. It's one of the distinct moments that I KNEW I was hearing God audibly.

Cameron shared that someone had told him they heard me discussing something he shared with me in confidence with my mom. I searched my memory, replaying conversations desperately trying to figure out who I would have had a conversation with. Genuinely confused and on a search within my mind, I heard clearly in my spirit: "Ask him who told him that."

So, I asked. He responded saying, "I can't tell you that." The Holy Spirit nudged me again: "Ask him who told him that." I persisted, telling Cameron I NEEDED him to tell me. He paused, dropped his head slightly, and turned towards Janet. "She told me", he said.

I remember losing all manner of couth. I broke. I cried profusely. I spoke from hurt. I couldn't understand how someone I had covered, defended, and stood by could lie so boldly. For Cameron to believe it easily enough to begin distancing himself from me took the cake. I was tired of people giving up on me so easily. I often felt like I contended for people, fought to understand them, tried to love them well, and to stay when things were hard. Yet somehow, I remained disposable in people's eyes. Elias asked Janet what she intended to gain from that conversation with Cameron? She had no answer.

After that night, the group slowly began to dissolve. Logan moved across the country. Janet became engaged and left the group shortly after. Cameron moved to another state. Eventually, only Elias, Sienna, and I remained. We agreed to finish the music we had invested in, but even that fell apart. We were working with a music mentor of mine in the studio during all of this, and it was agreed upon that we wouldn't waste what we had started.

However, those sentiments quickly changed between Sienna and Elias. Before I knew it, they requested a coffee shop meeting and informed me that they no longer wanted to pursue the group endeavor. I was blindsided but respected their decisions. I left the coffee shop that day and proceeded to call everyone who had invested monetarily in our project to inform them we would not be moving forward with it. That was one of the most embarrassing things I had ever done, but I had to do it. And I did it alone.

## The Double Down

After the dissolution of the group, Elias would still come by from time to time. Janet was about to get married, and I resolved that due to the nature of our relationship, I more than likely would not receive an invitation. There were people I had introduced Janet to who knew of our friendship and group dynamics, who would consistently ask if I was going to the wedding, to which I kindly replied that I wasn't sure, simply because I did not wish to disclose the nature of our group dynamics. As time grew closer to the ceremony, Janet eventually asked me to meet with her at her home to talk. She began to tell me that I did not receive an invitation because of the obvious distance between us, to which I understood.

Shortly after, Elias came by my home and in conversation, I asked him if he were ready for Janet's wedding. He gasped in exhaustion, saying he was "just ready to get it over with." For some reason, I asked him specifically what he was wearing, to which he informed me that Janet had requested he wear all black. I stated in response, "Oh! Well, she must have you doing something then!" To which Elias responded, no, she wasn't. I challenged him saying, "Elias, if she's asking you to wear a certain color, she'll definitely want you to do something specific." He disagreed. I was confused but left the conversation alone.

A few days after that exchange, I received an invitation in the mail to Janet's wedding. I prayed about if I should attend and resolved that I would go and support. The night before the wedding, Sienna called me to shoot the breeze. We had made it to an amicable point in our relationship and were able to have occasional small talk. Mid-conversation, she inserted that she, Elias, and Cameron were at Janet's rehearsal dinner, going over their host responsibilities. I truly believe she slipped up and revealed this information. I, however, remember the room stopping at a screeching halt. All I could think about was the conversation I had with Elias and how he denied having anything to do in the wedding. I told Sienna I needed to get off the phone and that I would see her the next day at the wedding. You could tell she was confused by my abrupt ending, but she obliged.

I called my mom and told her I had to be getting punked. It was yet another thing I had to stomach, and the night before the wedding felt cruel. I had already worked myself up to walk with my head high into an atmosphere where I didn't feel truly welcomed. I began to feel this was all set up to hurt me to my core. Everyone, including Sienna, whom Janet did not care for, was included in this wedding. Then to feel it was being hidden from me was yet another blow. The realization hit me hard.

The next day was the wedding day. I remember waking up and feeling a tremendous weight on my shoulders. It was heavy and draining. I knew I had to go and stand in the face of all that was happening, but it didn't stop the pain I was experiencing. I got in the shower and cried, asking the Lord if He saw me and all I was enduring.

I felt rejected, taunted, and emotionally beaten up, yet I still felt required to show up as if I weren't in pain. I remember thinking, " Is this what Jesus felt like when he had to bear his assignment and asked God to take the cup from Him? It was an agonizing pain. Grief, I suppose. I remember circulating thoughts of, "You're selfish. You're making this about you. If you're a Christian, you'll do what you have to do," surfacing over the pain. I pulled myself together, got out of the shower, got dressed, and prepared to go to the ceremony.

My aunt and mother accompanied me to the wedding. They were unwilling to let me go it alone, nor walk into a potentially challenging environment uncovered. As we rode in the car together, my aunt called my name from the backseat and said, "Maya, I just want you to know that *I SEE YOU*. I see what you're doing. It is teaching me so much, even as an elder in your life. Most Christians wouldn't have the courage to do what you're about to do. But you are teaching me what it looks like to overcome and stand against the enemy." She continued, "I just need you to know that *I SEE YOU* and I'm proud of you." I believe this was the first time that I experienced *EL ROI*. The God who sees us. It was too "coincidental" to not be God. As tears streamed down my face, I thanked her. She didn't know what I had just gone through that morning mentally and spiritually in the shower.

We pulled up to the church in my mom's Mercedes. Mom looked at me from the driver seat, strong and secure and said, "You ready?" I dried my tears to preserve my makeup and replied, "Yes ma'am." I got out of the car, and I turned "on". It was like a divine strength mixed with adrenaline switched on in me. I felt confident and capable. I hugged and greeted people I knew, took photos, and felt dazzling. As I walked into the church foyer, the first person there was Elias.

Something in me stopped. He reached out for a hug, and I kept walking. Not my best moment, but I went on to sign the guestbook across the room. As I signed the book, the Holy Spirit instructed me to go back, to which I did, and hugged him. I went into the ceremony, sat through it, and saw all of my former bandmates serving or included in some capacity. I attended the reception, danced, laughed, and wished Janet and her husband well. Sienna brought me home that night. When I walked through the threshold of my home, it was as if the adrenaline switch turned off. I took my shoes off in the foyer of our home and remember falling into the deepest depression I had ever experienced.

# Chapter 5: Bitter Roots

When I came home from that wedding, it was as if the final curtain had dropped on the performance I'd been holding up. I walked through the door, and everything in me went completely silent. The darkness wasn't dramatic; it was just heavy and immediate, like a quiet that settled and refused to leave. That night, I came home and did the only thing I felt I could do. I pulled on a hoodie, tugged the hood over my head, and slept the majority of next day away. It was as if I was trying to hide from the world under that fabric, wrapping myself in a cocoon of silence. But when I woke up, the weight was still there. Eventually, I remembered the advice people often give when you're feeling depressed: don't just stay in bed, don't close yourself off, try to get up, open the blinds, and find some small piece of normalcy.

So, I made myself go downstairs, where some close family friends were gathered. They knew the storm I was weathering, and they gave me space just to be. I sat in the room quietly, still with no words, just trying to breathe in a different space so I wouldn't drown in my own isolation. One of the women eventually turned to me and asked, "What's going on, Maya Moo?" That was her nickname for me. She was aware of all that had transpired. She was sensitive and intentional, offering me a gentle opening if I wanted to speak.

But the truth was, I felt so devastated and betrayed that I couldn't find the words. Every friend I trusted had turned away, and I was grappling with a grief that left me feeling utterly isolated. Her daughters, who also knew the weight of what I was going through, saw me sitting there in that silence. One of them asked if she could hug me, and when they both came and wrapped their arms around me, I broke. All the pain, the sense of betrayal, the feeling of being ostracized, all came spilling out in tears and an agonizing cry.

In the days that followed, I drifted through a haze. After that day of pulling my hoodie over my head and sinking into sleep, I moved through life like a shadow. Eventually, routine nudged me forward, and I found myself back inside the familiar walls of my parents' church for a Wednesday night Bible study. I debated whether I would even go. I had no desire for church. Still, something in me wanted to try. To see if the place that once felt like home might offer relief.

Worship had always been the place where I stood without thinking and where my voice came alive. But that day, my body wouldn't follow my memory. As worship and the Word went forth, I didn't stand. I didn't lift my hands. I slouched in a chair, disconnected. My posture and my silence told the story of a heart that felt profoundly let down. I had already experienced what it felt like to find a church home and lose it. I knew the shock of discovering a place that felt like home, only to have it pulled out from under me without warning. Another place I had trusted in, hoped for and believed I could stand. Gone.

At the time, I didn't even know to call bitterness by its name. I only knew how it felt. It felt like a heavy stone in my chest. Like a dull ache that colored everything gray. It was the quiet anger of feeling abandoned and the unspoken grief of shattered dreams. A sense of betrayal that came from feeling like I'd been faithful and still ended up wounded. At this point, most of the pain I'd experienced had come through the hands of people in ministry. People I believed were part of God's plan for my life. I had been courageous enough to ask for this group, thinking I was doing exactly what The Lord was asking of me. To find myself here, feeling like I'd been set up for heartbreak, in the name of God, made that wound even deeper.

It shook my trust in God. I began to believe that all that I had known about God was a lie. That he was not Good. Because I couldn't fathom how every single thing He had given to my family and me would leave us with nothing but brokenness we had to attempt to piece back together.

I was angry, because I watched how my mother was set up and the same depression I began to experience, I saw her experience. The same way I'd lie in bed, feeling like the wind was knocked out of me, was the same thing I nursed my mom out of. It was debilitating. I remember my dad questioning if he had made a mistake by finding our former church home and if he had subjected us to that level of spiritual abuse. The effects of those blows ate at my parents' confidence and their hearts. I now found myself questioning my own decisions. In my heart, I believed God allowed it to happen. I questioned what kind of God I had signed my life up for. Surely, He couldn't be a good one, and there was nothing that could convince me otherwise.

I struggled with His character, so much so that things that naturally connected me to him like music, faded within me. I didn't stop listening to music intentionally. I didn't decide to walk away from worship. I just stopped reaching for it. I no longer enjoyed nor connected to it. It would lie in me, wanting to come out, but I was blocked. Maybe by all that my body, mind and spirit had experienced. That prison held me for years and the realization came unexpectedly. Someone played a worship song I didn't recognize about 4 years after all of the events, and they asked if I'd heard it yet. I hadn't. They mentioned the artist. I didn't know the name. The song had been out long enough that my not knowing stood out, even to me. I was always in the know concerning God, church, and all things worship. I enjoyed it all, so being blithely unaware wasn't like me. As the child who could sing before she could talk, music wasn't something I enjoyed; it was how I breathed. It was how I prayed. It was how I processed God. And without consciously choosing it, bitterness had muted that part of me.

People asked me for years, time and time again, if I was singing. Every time, something in me would cringe. It felt like an open wound, tender and unhealed, aching the moment someone brushed against it. I learned how to navigate around the questions and land on answers that felt safe enough to offer without exposing the truth. But safety came at a cost. Each deflection was also a quiet denial of the very gifts I carried. What people couldn't see was that I couldn't answer without telling the whole story. I couldn't explain my silence without naming the wounds beneath it. I hadn't only become musically quiet; I had gone mute altogether. I lived inside my own internal processing system, where everything stayed contained and unresolved. Nothing came out of me, at least not without strain. And when something did surface, it was laced with insecurity, fear, and apprehension. My freedom was restrained.

From the outside, it may have looked like hesitation. Even disobedience. I'm sure it looked like wasted potential. It surely felt that way. But what was actually happening was far more complicated. I wasn't merely resisting my gift. I was protecting myself from reopening something I didn't yet know how to tend to. My silence and dormancy weren't the absence or ignorance of calling; it was the evidence of pain. And pain, when misunderstood, is often misnamed.

# Chapter 6: Mishandling the Wounded

People often assume that when someone isn't operating in their gift, it's because they've grown complacent or fearful, or because they've somehow turned away from what God has called them to do. From the outside, silence gets interpreted as avoidance, retreat gets labeled as disobedience, and stillness is mistaken for a lack of faith. I battled the pressure to perform while feeling immense pain. It was as if my entire existence relied on and was validated solely by my output. But all I desired to do was be still. Transparently, I felt as if I literally couldn't move. This wrestling often made me feel like I had failed, and worse, that I was a failure. If God was so good, why couldn't I just get up and move forward as if nothing had happened? Along with grappling with grave disappointment, internal shame grew within me about not showing up. But Scripture gave me a different story about people who found themselves in similar predicaments.

Again and again, God's people are shown retreating, hiding, or going quiet, not because the calling was gone, but because the cost of carrying it had become too heavy in that season. There are accounts of prophets who fled, leaders who withdrew, servants who questioned their capacity, and people who needed distance before they could reengage. However, unlike people, Scripture does not rush to condemn them for it. I often felt ashamed, as if I had dropped my spiritual ball after engaging in certain conversations with Christians. But I learned that Scripture makes room for the reality of retreat far more than we, the Church, often do.

For example, after the crucifixion, the disciples did not regroup publicly. They hid. John's Gospel is explicit: *"The doors were locked for fear of the Jews."* (John 20:19). These were men who had walked with Jesus, preached with authority, and witnessed miracles. Yet, after trauma and loss, they retreated.

Scripture does not spiritualize their fear. It names it. And Jesus' response matters. When Jesus appeared among them, He did not demand courage. He did not ask why they weren't outside proclaiming resurrection. His first words were not correction or commission. They were, *"Peace be with you."* He met them in hiding before calling them back into the world.

Thomas represents another kind of retreat. The church often labels Thomas as "doubting". I've always held an issue with that label because of the context of his encounter with Jesus. After the crucifixion, he withdrew. Not physically, but relationally and spiritually. He refused belief without evidence. He withheld trust. And when Jesus encountered him, He did not shame him for skepticism born of loss. He invited him closer saying, *"Put your finger here."* I have often wondered why Christians rarely focus on the fact that Jesus allowed Thomas to engage the wound before asking him to believe again. He was not offended by Thomas' doubt. He met him in it.

The women who followed Jesus also retreated after the crucifixion. Scripture tells us they went to the tomb in grief and confusion, not expectation. Even when confronted with resurrection, they initially responded with fear and silence. Mark's Gospel records, *"They said nothing to anyone, for they were afraid."* (Mark 16:8). Fear muted their voices. And still, Jesus entrusted them with the message.

Finally, we have the great prophet Elijah. Elijah had completed a series of miraculous feats back-to-back. He faced 450 prophets of Baal on Mount Carmel, called down fire from heaven, and prayed until a drought broke. Elijah stood boldly against Jezebel and was deeply grieved when he realized she would double down in her pursuit to kill him, even after all he had done under the direction and power of God.

Elijah, afraid, is found in 1 Kings hiding in a cave, deeply distressed and asking God to let him die. He is absolutely spent and clearly feels like a failure. Elijah is found lamenting, *"for I am no better than my fathers.*" But what I find beautiful and telling is that in Elijah's distress, the Lord, before commissioning him to go out again, first allowed him to lie down. He allowed him to sleep. Scripture tells us that ravens brought him food to strengthen him for forty days and forty nights until the brook dried up.

Then the Lord appeared in 1 Kings 19:9 and asks, *"What are you doing here, Elijah?"* I am of the belief that there is no question the Lord has ever asked in the Word that He does not know the answer to. The Lord gave Elijah the space to voice his fears, disappointments, and disorientation. He was utterly in despair after doing everything God had asked of him. He said, *"I have been very zealous for the Lord God of hosts."* In essence he was saying, "I've been faithful to You, and this is how it ends for me?" The Lord responds to this by immediately giving Elijah his next assignment. However, I believe it's important to recognize that the next assignment did NOT come before Elijah is given room to FEEL.

These stories make room for a powerful truth: God does not always commission us before He strengthens us. That was the misperception I lived inside while I was hiding myself. I was not merely hiding. God's mercy, attention and healing were meeting me in the place of pain. Jesus did not interpret retreat as failure, nor did He equate fear with faithlessness. He did not demand immediate return to function. Instead, He can be found meeting people exactly where they were. Behind locked doors, in doubt, in grief, in the margins, and in caves.

Scripture never says The Lord praises hiding, but it clearly shows instances where He did not punish it. He treated it as human, understandable, and often as a response to pain. And that matters because it reveals hiding as evidence of survival and an opportunity for the hand of the Lord to meet you.

# Chapter 7: Found in Retreat

In 2018, I found myself at an impasse. I was working in advertising, but I had taken time to reflect on what I truly wanted and desired. The group I had once been committed to had completely broken down. My faith was rebuilding itself, but I still felt fragile. I remember showing up to work and feeling empty, as if I were forcing myself through days that no longer fit. All I wanted was to move toward things that made me feel alive again, things I had always wanted to do but had pushed aside for the sake of stability, loyalty, or expectation

A part of me had been consumed by so many things for so long that when I lost what I had committed myself to, a strange kind of clarity set in. That's another thing about pain and grief. They sober you. They wake you up to what has been taking more than it gives mentally, spiritually, and physically. And once you see that clearly, it's hard to unsee it.

I had always done hair. Since the age of thirteen. It wasn't just something I picked up. It was something that lived in me. Going to cosmetology school had been on my bucket list for years. I had dreams of opening a salon, maybe even a school one day. And in 2018, I found myself craving the things that brought me joy. I needed an outlet. I needed something that belonged to me. But going back to school meant leaving my full-time job, and that scared me.

It was the first job I landed right after finishing undergrad. I was the first intern ever be hired full time, and the only African American employee to be offered a position in the way I was. It was a big deal. And yet, about nine months in, I began recognizing signs that it wasn't the best fit for me. So, I was faced with a decision to make. In February of 2018, I put in my notice of resignation and gave the company a three-month window, something I still can't believe they honored. I planned to begin cosmetology school in June of that same year. Many people at the company tried to talk me out of it. Some literally told me that it wouldn't be a successful move and questioned my decision. But twenty-five-year-old me had a quiet resolve. Giving that extended notice of resignation gave me time to adjust, breathe, and prepare.

When the three months ended, hesitation crept in. I don't remember a specific reason. I just remember something not feeling fully settled within me. That sensing prompted me to push my start date back to October. When October came, and it came fast, I found myself in a completely new environment: a full-time cosmetology student. I knew I wanted to finish. I knew this mattered. But if I'm honest, I couldn't make sense of my path. It felt disjointed and unclear, like my life had taken an unexpected turn that I hadn't prepared for. Still, something in me sensed that God would use it. I just didn't understand how yet.

### First Day of School

I remember showing up to school dressed in all black. That was the uniform. All black from head to toe.  I was escorted into a classroom for our institute-wide opening session and instantly felt like a kindergartener. The room was buzzing. Hundreds of students in uniform moved with nervous energy. The space itself was stark. White walls, mirrors lining every side, and concrete floors beneath our feet. Most of the students were women, younger than me, many of them coming straight out of high school and into cosmetology school as their next step. I resonated with that decision deeply. That had once been my plan too. But growing up with a father in academia meant pursuing an undergraduate degree was mandatory, so my path towards this goal took longer to circle back.

That first day, I had already decided something internally. I wasn't there to make friends. I had a goal. Come to class, accumulate my 1,500 clock hours, graduate, and take my licensure exam. That was it. I wasn't interested in opening myself up. I was still recovering from loss, and I didn't have the emotional margin for unnecessary attachment.

During our opening session, which they called a "huddle", the principal gave his remarks. I don't remember every word, but I remember specific statements.

*"You are here on purpose."*
*"You will change lives, but your life will be changed too,"*
*"It's not by accident that you're here."*

I left that huddle with chills. Those words didn't feel generic. They felt personal, as if the Lord was using that moment to confirm something to me. The most frustrating part of my life at that point was the lack of clarity. I struggled with not knowing how everything was supposed to make sense and connect. How did I go from this to that? And where is this taking me? My trust muscle was depleted. Every time I felt settled in the past, something shifted. Interrupted. Dismantled. Over time, that pattern became deeply discouraging. It made me wonder if I was ever truly on track, or if I kept missing something. Those opening statements softened that fear. They told me I could rest here and that I wasn't off course.

After huddle, we were separated into our cohorts. The structure was similar to a graduate program. You matriculated with the same group, with the hope of finishing together. I remember realizing I was one of only two African American women in my cohort. The other African American woman was a bit older than me, quiet and reserved. I decided immediately that I wasn't going to be her friend. Furthermore, I wasn't going to be her friend because we were the only two black girls in the class. I still laugh about that now, but I can see it for what it was. My longing for a relationship was trying its hardest to peek through the walls I had carefully built.

For the first month, I focused on staying locked in on my studies. I engaged without over-exposing myself. My priority was finishing. Even in my hiding, encouragement kept finding me.

I recall an instance with my first instructor. He was a militant, bald, extremely fit Black man who ran the classroom like we were preparing for war. He surveyed our work with precision and held the highest expectations for how we carried ourselves and executed our work. When I entered school, I intentionally never mentioned that I had already accumulated cosmetology hours in high school. I never talked about the clientele I had built back then or carried through undergrad. I wanted to learn earnestly. I also didn't want to be pushed to the forefront. I had learned that sometimes being seen meant being expected to carry more. I was unwilling to put that pressure on myself.

One day, he stopped at my station and examined my work. I stepped back, away from my mannequin, and allowed him to inspect it. To my surprise, and I believe his too, He didn't adjust anything. Instead, "Oh!," he said. Almost surprised. "You're built for this,", he remarked. And he moved on. That affirmation landed with me in more ways than one. At that point in my life, I didn't feel built at all. I felt broken down. But those small moments of encouragement, precise and unexpected, kept soothing my heart like a world-renowned surgeon using His skill on a case only He could tend to.

Around the second month, the other African American woman in my cohort and I began making small talk. Her name was Harmonie. She was a wife, a mother, and worked in the medical field. She would come to school after a twelve-hour hospital shift and still commit to eight hours at cosmetology school. Her grit astounded me.

She later told me she had also seen me on the first day and decided she wasn't going to be my friend either, simply because I was the only other Black woman in the class. That became a hilarious connection point for us. What made it even more meaningful was discovering that she, too, had planned to start in the summer and delayed until October. It became clear that God was orchestrating our timing.

Harmonie didn't have sisters, and I was coming out of painful experiences in the area of sisterhood and friendship. We found one another in the middle of one of the most demanding, transitional seasons of our lives. Cosmetology school required everything from us. Tenacity, commitment, skill, and endurance. We quickly became each other's shoulders, not just in school, but in life.

One day at lunch, Harmonie asked how I ended up there. It was the first time I had told someone outside of my family everything that had led me to that place. We sat in my Kia Optima, eating our mozzarella sticks from Sonic, and she listened. Without judgment and without trying to edit my experience or rushing me to get over it. She held space for my fragility and wouldn't allow me to skim over the pain I had experienced, which was something I was good at.

That was new for me, because I had learned to self-sacrifice by way of withholding the full truth; everything appearing fine on the outside. I often covered for those who had harmed me. Harmonie showed me that safety didn't require performance. She affirmed that God had me, even when I couldn't see it clearly myself. That day, I found a sister and an advocate. Both things I so desperately needed.

Slowly, that school became a place of safety and a place where the Lord continually met me. One day, as I walked toward the front desk to check client assignments, an old college classmate, someone I had spent significant time serving alongside, walked in to be serviced. I hadn't seen her in years.

She looked at me and exclaimed, "What are you doing here?" "I'm in school," I responded. I hadn't publicly announced that I had left my corporate job. I was nervous about her response. But to my surprise, her face lit up. "You are exactly where you're supposed to be," she said with conviction. I felt ease wash over my body. That God-affirming thing again.

Those moments kept happening with classmates and with clients. I would stand over people preparing them for service, and conversations would unfold that felt like ministry. Not just me to them, but them to me. It was as if the Lord had hand-picked each person I encountered to help rebuild me from the inside out. I wasn't getting paid. I didn't have a job. I was in school full-time, giving everything I had. I was paying off my tuition with money I was earning on the side from clientele. Looking back, I was stretched. And yet, I felt full. Exhausted, but loved. Tired, but seen. By making one commitment to pivot into the uncertain, the Lord met me there. Applying balm to every wound I carried and quietly rebuilding what had been broken

### Nearing The Finish

The Cosmetology program was eighteen months long, and it was a long, grueling eighteen months. By month four, I was onto the second level in the program, the equivalent of a sophomore in college.

One day, a front desk staff member came to speak with my instructor, requesting Harmonie and me specifically. Two patrons were asking for services that were well above the skill level of most students at the institute. We were asked to service them. Technically, we did not yet have the hours required to be on the salon floor under Tennessee State Board regulations. But we were summoned.

I remember feeling a hidden resentment. Not because I couldn't do the work, but because I was being pulled to do it. There is a strange comfort in placing yourself on reserve. Looking back, I can see that hiding to heal had shifted into a quiet rebellion. I had given myself freely before, and it drained me. It left me alone and empty. So, this time, I had unconsciously decided I would dispense parts of myself on my own terms.

I do believe there is a hiding and covering that God allows. I like to think of it as insulation. Insulation exists to regulate what passes through. It protects what's inside from being damaged by conditions outside, preserving stability until the structure is strong enough to stand on its own. In the same way, there are seasons when God places a covering over us, shielding our identity, our gifts, or our calling from exposure before the proper time. That kind of covering is not the same as hiding in fear or rebelling in retreat. Hiding in fear shrinks us back from purpose and creates a rebellion that resists the process altogether. That's where I found myself when called upon. Resistant and unwilling, desiring to move at my own pace and on my own terms.

As I mentioned in the previous chapter, the Prophet Elijah's story taught me much about hiding places. When he fled to hide in the mountain after enduring trial after trial, assignment after assignment, utterly exhausted, that was a period of retreat that the Lord allowed and provided for. But that period had a timestamp on it. A divine end date. Being pulled from that class was the Lord saying, "Time's Up. I have something for you to do. You're needed."

Cosmetology school stretched me in ways I hadn't expected it to. To this day, having obtained a Bachelor's, Master's, and Cosmetology license, I tell people that Cosmetology school was by far the hardest thing I had ever done. Because every single day, I had to make the intentional decision to resist my own reluctance. That atmosphere was God-ordained, and it taught me a valuable lesson about not showing up. Every day I chose not to show up pushed my completion date back. I watched classmates fall into delinquency. So far behind that they either had to restart their coursework entirely or drop out of the program altogether. Not showing up was a costly decision.

There were days when life happened. I experienced sickness, my grandmother passed away, and some days I simply had no energy. But the goal was clear: 1500 hours to the finish, and I was determined to complete them. Every day I missed, I made it up immediately.

What I learned in that season is something I carry with me even now: rest has a purpose, and sometimes God allows a season of covering and insulation for your recovery. But every day beyond the rest He has ordained begins to cost you. Delay stretches the journey, hesitation postpones completion, and hiding past the appointed time slowly robs you of what was meant to be finished sooner. There is a difference between the insulation God provides for a season and the absence we choose for ourselves. One preserves you. The other postpones you.

When I reached the master's level of the program, I was on track to graduate on time, even with the setbacks. One day, I was alone in the color room, cleaning out my tools, when my first instructor, the tall, bald, African American man who had once told me, "I was built for this", found me there. He stood in the doorway and looked at me. He had a way of looking at you that felt as if he were reading your internal world.

"You're bored, aren't you?" he asked. Honestly, I was beyond bored. "I'm just ready to finish," I replied.

By that point, I was a Level 3 master's student, nearing the fifteen hundred hours required to complete the program and take my state board examination. It was the equivalent of being a senior in college. What set me apart was my skill level. I had surpassed that level of instruction.

When he asked if I was bored, he wasn't guessing. He could see that I was doing my best to maneuver through a level I had already mastered. "I can tell you're bored," he said. "You've exceeded this level. You actually exceeded it a long time ago," he continued. I humbly nodded my head as I continued cleaning in the color room.

But he wasn't finished. His eyes were pierced and focused on mine. It was as if he had to continue. And he did.

"When you leave here, you're not going to be able to take the traditional route most of the other students will take to develop. **You** won't be able to take that route. You are already ahead of the game." I nodded again, taking in every word. Then we parted ways.

A few months later, it was graduation day. I remember getting dressed, grateful to use my graduation privileges to skip the all-black uniform. When I arrived at school, I went through our normal morning programming. At the master's level, you would typically check your schedule on the monitors to prepare for your client load for the day.

That day, my books were completely blocked off. It was a gesture reserved for students nearing their 1500-hour mark. As the final hour approached, my classmates and instructors gathered on and around the stairwell where a large, shiny gong hung at the top. With hairspray in hand, my classmates cheered as I climbed the stairs. When I reached the top, relief washed over me. I lifted the mallet and struck the gong. The echo rang across the open salon floor. I had finished what I had set out to do.

As I walked back down through a cloud of hairspray my classmates had created, I was met at the bottom of the stairs by clients, instructors, friends, and family. The overwhelming sense of love was almost disorienting. They congratulated me, embraced me, and spoke kind words over my life. One moment in particular has stayed with me.

My master's instructor, Chad, was the last to hug me. Chad was like a dad/big brother to many of us. He created an atmosphere where fear and anxiety could loosen their grip, which is rare in a high-stakes master's level cosmetology program. He waited patiently while everyone else sent me off. When he finally hugged me, he held me tightly and whispered, "I'm so proud of you. You're so special. Go out and preach the Word, my dear. No more hiding. You're needed." I was overwhelmed by those sentiments. They were so specific. Chad and I had never had an in-depth conversation about God or ministry. Yet he spoke directly into something I had been trying to bury.

I learned something that day that has stayed with me ever since. What it truly looks like to be **marked.** When you are marked, it doesn't matter where you go. It doesn't matter where you hide, what detours you take or what routes you choose. **Who you are and whose you are will always be noticed.** Furthermore, the Lord will place people in your life, especially when you think you are hiding well, to say, "I see exactly who you are," even if you're trying not to be seen."

# Chapter 8: Divine Call Outs

The moment with Chad made me think of other times in my life when the Lord was divinely calling me out. I remember working at the advertising agency, and one of the brand managers sent me an unexpected text message on the clock. We weren't extremely close, but we would engage in workplace banter often. We had just finished up a series of back-and-forths in a very unserious email thread. My phone chimed, and I saw a text from her that read, "Also, off the work email record, I've had a premonition of you being a pastor. Do you preach at your church? Because it's your gift, I think (No pressure)." I remember smiling slightly, because at the time, my parents had started a church, and I was serving as a youth minister. I let her know that in my reply.

I recall the feeling that came over me. It felt like exposure, but not in a negative way. It felt more like a revealing, like a veil being lifted at the right time.  I remember looking up the word premonition. As a church girl, you're taught early on to never casually play with spiritual language. But I wanted to understand the word and see how it aligned with what I already sensed. A premonition is an early warning or anticipation of a future event. I believe her spiritual foundation, which was not Christian, gave her the closest word she had to describe what she was sensing about me. But even at twenty-four, I knew that what she called a premonition was really the Holy Spirit pointing out His own.

The "gut feeling" she had, whether she realized it or not, was the Spirit of the Living God telling her, **"That one? She's mine."**

What made the moment so beautiful was that the Lord compelled her enough to say something. He used her voice so that my spirit could connect with what He was trying to communicate to me. That was also my first introduction into how the Lord will use anyone to get to you. A lesson that was further solidified in Cosmetology school.

Some religious people might have dismissed what she said because of her word choice. But something settled in me. I felt led to discern beyond religiosity. The Lord was calling me out, the same way He did with Chad in cosmetology school. The same way He did with my instructor when I first walked through the doors to begin my 1,500 clock hours. I would continue to learn that this is characteristic of a Father who knows, sees, and tracks His children.

### Marked

My mother has often told me a story about when my siblings and I were first born. She recounts something my father did immediately after each of our births. As she tells it, my dad was adamant about being the first to hold each of us. Before nurses could administer anything or barely wipe us off, he would take us to the side of the room and dedicate us back to the Lord.

That story has always held deep significance for me. I believe it offers a physical picture of what it means to be marked by God.

To be marked is for someone to stake a claim on you. It is similar to carrying a family name. Wherever you go, whoever you encounter, there is an understanding that you are connected to something larger than yourself. A name carries reputation, legacy, and identity. We have all known people whose names carry weight and others whose names carry a less favorable reputation. Being marked by God is very similar to this experience. Those who are unaware or unwilling to accept that they are marked often struggle with the implications of it. I certainly did for a while. What I have learned is that when God places His mark on your life, it does not only shape who you are. It also defines what you must carry.

## The Cost of Being Marked

At first, being marked by God feels like a privilege. I remember being a child and constantly being told that I was special. That God had a calling on my life. That the Lord would do amazing things with me. That many people would be impacted by my life. At face value, being special in the eyes of God felt amazing. It made me feel like I truly was something to behold. It made me feel seen in a way I often did not feel as a middle child, or as someone who stood out but was not always included.

But as I grew older and experiences compounded, something shifted. I developed a resentment toward being marked. I began to associate it with usefulness rather than relationship. I started to believe I was valuable only because of what I could produce for other people, and even for God.

I grew weary of the trials that seemed to accompany that identity. I watched my family suffer at the hands of people God had seemingly called into our lives, and it took a toll on my belief. Being marked began to feel like a burden rather than a blessing. Even as I write this, I am yet on a journey of reshaping my understanding of what it means to be marked by God in a way that does not center suffering as its defining feature.

More than anything, I have learned that attempting to avoid being marked creates grave misalignment. When we resist the current of what God has placed on our lives, fighting our identity rather than leaning into it, He will beckon us to slow down long enough to learn this valuable truth: **being marked does not only mean we will be *used*. Being marked also means we will be *held*.** It means we are in the palm of His hand and under His precise and loving care. I did not always see it that way. For a long time, I believed being marked meant God would use me, allow others to use me, and discard me once His purpose was accomplished. But Scripture says that He stands at the door of our hearts and knocks. His knocking is persistent because **He wants you**. He doesn't simply desire to use you.

That is the truth I'm learning to believe. No matter how much I try to ignore it, the pull toward God will never stop as long as I (we) are breathing His air. It calls to you day and night, not merely toward what you are meant to do, but toward who you are meant to **be** with Him. It settles in your chest and deep in your gut, waiting patiently for you to acknowledge that it is there. The life of a marked individual is not best lived in resistance, but in surrender. Not solely because of what God may do through you, but because of the relationship He desires to have ***with*** you.

# Chapter 9: Out of Hiding

*"And oh as you run, what hindered love will only become part of the story."*
*-Steffany Gretzinger, Amanda Cook*

As I write this book, I have reached the point where it is time to come out of hiding. Throughout this process, the Lord has given me a vision of myself on a rollercoaster. I've gotten on the ride, buckled myself in, and it has ticked and trudged slowly up the angled side of the track. The track is life. Exhaustion and fear have often joined me on the ride, often causing me to wonder if I'll survive the remainder of it. But anticipation and exhilaration have joined me at this stage of the ride.

From this height, I've been able to see things from a different perspective. As I've been pulled tighter into the ride, I've grown more comfortable in my seat. My grip has loosened as fear begins to release, and I have taken inventory of everything I have experienced up to this point.

And now, I'm at the edge of this part of the track, my seat slightly tilting over the curve. What's ahead feels like a rush of fresh sights, new momentum, and a push into the next stage of the ride. At this point, there's no turning back. This momentum is now driven by the reality and acceptance of being marked. And I believe that's where you are, too.

If you have made it this far in the book, I believe you have been in a season of hiding. What may have started as a season of healing may have quietly become an extended period of concealing yourself for one reason or another. I believe your appointed time of healing has expired, and now, God is calling you. He is beckoning you back into your **rightful place**.

It can feel almost frustrating how that inner pulling refuses to leave you alone. But I am here to tell you, it will not. It is time to get back on the ride. And the beautiful thing is, you are ready now. Not ready because you are perfectly prepared, but ready because you have resolved that it is better to be aligned than to remain off course another day. Ready because you are willing to take a bet on God again and trust that He is big enough to hold you.

My prayer is that you would come to peace with the truth that your story has included challenges, disappointments, setbacks, discouragement, betrayal, heartbreak, and disillusionment. And I pray that you would recognize that none of it is enough to make you quit on yourself or on the plan God has for your life—a life meant to prosper you, not to harm you.

If you are anything like me in this season, coming out of hiding will not be loud. For me, it feels tender and sacred, mixed with the vulnerability of stepping into unfamiliar territory. It feels like learning how to move again without flinching. But this time, we are not starting from scratch. We are starting from experience.

We permit ourselves to lean into all that we are again. Permission to create. Permission to explore. Permission to be curious. To try without needing our validation to come from the outcome. To let joy be useful, even if it does not look impressive.

Coming out of hiding means reclaiming our power and our presence in a way that says, I am here, and I am not abandoning myself this time. It means resting in the One who marks our souls, the Lord, rather than striving to hold everything together on our own. It means stepping back into the journey, trusting that whatever comes, we will be sustained. There is no need to cover what the Lord already sees. Coming out of hiding is freedom from concealing what was never meant to be hidden. Our power is no longer something we strive to grasp. It is something we return to, rooted in trust in the One who sustains us, and in the selves we are finally learning to honor.

I pray you would allow yourself to step into this journey, one step at a time. May the Lord meet you in each step. And may you discover that as you run, everything that once hindered you has become **part** of your story, not the end of it.

# About The Author

**Maya Robinson** is a writer, creative, and faith-driven leader passionate about helping others move from retreat into purpose. Through her work, she explores the intersection of vulnerability, spiritual growth, and personal transformation, inviting readers to confront fear, embrace healing, and live fully seen.

Her debut memoir, *Out of Hiding*, chronicles her journey from shrinking to surrender, weaving together personal story and spiritual insight with honesty and depth. Maya believes that hiding may be a survival response, but it is never a permanent home.

She holds a Master of Professional Studies in Coaching and Strategic Leadership from Lipscomb University, where she also earned a certification in Coaching, and a Bachelor of Business Administration in Marketing from Tennessee State University. A licensed cosmetologist since 2019, Maya's creative background uniquely informs her appreciation for identity, confidence, and the power of personal expression.

Based in Nashville, Tennessee, she continues to create spaces (both on the page and in community) where authenticity, faith, and growth are not only encouraged, but embodied.

**This is not where it ends.**

If these pages met you in a real place…
if something in you was seen, softened, or stirred…
I want you to know, this wasn't by accident.

There is more unfolding.
More becoming.
More of you waiting to be fully embodied.

*And you don't have to navigate that alone.*

If you feel led to stay connected, I've created spaces beyond this
book for us to continue the journey together.

**You can find me here:**
**Website: www.themayarob.com**
**Instagram: @themayarob**

*Thank you for allowing this book to meet you. I'd be so grateful if
you shared your experience in a review on Amazon.*

Your words help this message reach the people it's meant for.

*-Maya*